FLEET

A
THRILLING ADVENTURE IN SPACE

# SPACE FLEET

## A THRILLING ADVENTURE IN SPACE

By Michael Thomson
Illustrations by Neil Sutton

LDA

SPACE FLEET
LD 868(ii)
ISBN 1 85503 036 5

First published 1989

LDA Duke Street, Wisbech, Cambs PE13 2AE, England

# SPACE FLEET

You are the star of this Space Adventure! Only you can be the ace Space Pilot and make a hyper-space jump to find new planets.

To read Space Fleet you need a copy of the Adventure Sheet on the last page of this book. (You can write in the book if it is your own. If not ask someone to photocopy it for you.) You also need a pencil and two dice.

You will meet many strange things on your adventure to the stars. Sometimes you will need to fight them. To fight throw your dice and see how many Fighting Skill Points you have. If you have the same or more than your enemy you win. If you have less Points than your enemy, you lose. The story will tell you when to fight, and what happens next.

Look at your Adventure Sheet. It lists all the things you may have to fight. You may not meet them in this order. Each time you fight, fill in your Adventure Sheet.

Your Adventure Sheet also shows you that you have 25 Life Points. You might lose Life Points on your adventure. You might also be given some more. Be careful, if you lose all your Life Points you die!

On your Adventure Sheet there is an Equipment List. You will be given many useful things on your journey. Remember to write them on your Equipment List.

When you finish reading, write down the number you are on. Do this in the Story Number column on your Adventure Sheet. Then you will know where to start next time.

As you read this book you will meet many new and strange things. Some of them have odd names. If you do not know what they mean, look at your Space Glossary at the back of the book.

# SPACE FLEET

## 1

You are in a deep sleep. You are on the spaceship Titan. It is the Flagship of the Space Fleet! The Fleet is going to make a hyper-space jump. The Fleet is going to look for other planets. There are many people who are going to look for new places to live on. You have been posted to be one of the Fighter Ship Pilots. You can read about this in the book "Space Pilot!"

You wake up. At first you do not know where you are. Then it all comes back to you. You can hear a sharp screech in the intercom. It is a signal to wake you up. You pick up the intercom. You are told to go at once to the Captain.

You wash the sleep out of your eyes. Then you set off to the control room. Just as you go out of the door of the cabin you run into someone. It is a Space Pilot. He says "Look out you stupid fool!"

You try to tell him that you are sorry but he will not take any notice. He looks as if he has been a Space Pilot for some years. He looks at you again, "So you are the great new pilot," he sneers "so great that you think you can run into anyone. Just because you got the best marks at Space School. Well, here that stands for nothing."

He does not seem to like you very much! He dares you to meet him in a contest. If you will take up his dare to a space duel go to 47, if you do not want to take up the dare go to 88.

## 2

You head out to the blips. The spaceships close in — 38.

## 3

You go near to the GAS GIANT. You feel the huge force of gravity pull the ship in. The radar shows that you are near something in space. Spod picks up a message. It is an old message. It has been sending the same thing for a long time. The message is in code. Spod makes a record of it. You will take it back to the Fleet. Write down "OLD MESSAGE" on your Equipment List.

Then you find that the ship is being taken down into the planet. The gravity of the huge planet is too great for you. You may be crushed to death on the surface of the planet. You have one chance. Throw your dice and work out your Fighting Skill Points — 7.

## 4

You move away. The two ships flash past each other! — 35.

## 5

The hum from the box gets softer. You are moving away from Mass/gravity. Go back to 115 and move again.

## 6

You leave the Fleet. The BLACK SHAPE burns up half the Fleet. Lose 5 Life Points. The rest of your Fighter Force tell you that you must attack. Go to 50.

## 7

You will try to fling the ship around the planet. You will have to go full speed. You will have to make your power thrust at the right time.

GAS GIANT GRAVITY
FIGHTING SKILL 7

If you win — 32. If you lose — 101.

## 8

The comet is too fast. You have to let down the thrust. You will overheat. The comet goes off into space. You return to the Fleet. It is about to move off — 117.

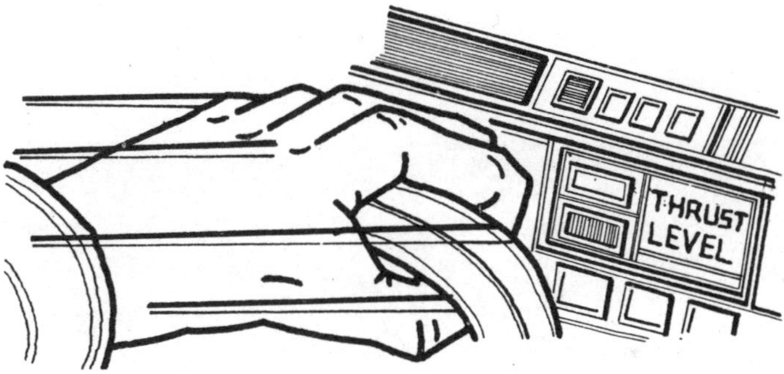

## 9

You send a Human to look at it. She comes back and says, "There is a hole, like a plug, in the side of the BLACK SHAPE." Now what? — 92.

## 10

You find nothing. You are lost in Null-space for all time.

## 11

The Ril will not go on their own. They say that they will be killed. Why don't Humans risk it? The BLACK SHAPE sends a laser blast while you talk. Lose 1 Life Point — 83.

## 12

You choose the Protect Fighter Force. You report to the Commander — 41.

## 13

The BLACK HOLE pulls at the ships. The ships try to get away.

THE BLACK HOLE
FIGHTING SKILL 14

If you win — 87. If you lose — 113.

## 14

You feel very sick. The REPTILE is coming at you. Lose 2 Life Points. You will have to fight it. You can only use ONE of the dice for your Fighting Skills. You have no CAT FORCE and are not strong. Work out your Fighting Skill Points (ONE dice!) go to 45.

## 15

You have the MESSAGE. What will you do with it? If you have the MESSAGE CONTROL — 21, if you do not — 105.

## 16

You send one of the other pilots to look at the comet. When he gets back he says that he could not get to the comet. It was going too fast. The Fleet then begins to move out — 117.

## 17

You go back to the main Fleet — 36.

## 18

You tell Aaan that it is foolish to risk your ships. You lose the race. You also lose 2 Life Points. Now go to 114.

## 19

You put the Ril and Human ships into small units. The ships move all around the BLACK SHAPE. Then you tell all the ships in the first wave to attack from all sides. The BLACK SHAPE can only shoot down so many. You hope to get past its guns. The first wave fires its lasers. Some hit the SHAPE. The SHAPE fires. It just fires anywhere. You send the second wave in. You are in the second wave. Aaan shouts, "Over the top! Stick 'em up! Shoot 'em down buster! Crack an egg! Yahoo!" She thinks that these are all Earth sayings. You do not tell her that they are all old sayings. Spod says "Crack an egg?". Throw your dice and work out your Fighting Skill Points — 30.

## 20

You turn on the Speed Kit. You tell Spod to man the lasers. He is not happy but does as you say. You move at attack speed to the Ril ships. Too late you find out that there are many ships. Four of their Fighters break off and box you in. A voice in Rilish says, "You are foolish Pilot. Call your Commander!" Take 2 Life Points off your Life Points Score. You then call Commander Hibbs — 91.

## 21

You have the MESSAGE CONTROL. You feed the MESSAGE into the ship's controls. The blue face inside the BLACK SHAPE robot told you to do this. You see numbers and letters print out on the screen. It is the code of a star. It tells you how to get there. It gives you the way into hyper-space. Some say that the Fleet must not go there. The 'enemy' that the blue face talked about may be there. Others say that this means there will be life there. The 'enemy' may not be there any more — 33.

## 22

Wrong code! The BLACK SHAPE hits you. Lose 3 Life Points — 94.

## 23

You choose the Scout Fighter Force. Report to the Commander — 41.

## 24

You move away. The two ships flash past each other! — 35.

## 25

You go to the warm planet. This is not too far from the sun. It is not too close. It seems like Earth in our own Solar System. Spod looks at the read-out from the computer scan. "There is water here" he says. "There is also gas to breathe. Oxygen and gases like Earth's are here."

You think that this can be a good planet for Humans (and Ril!). You land. You get out of the ship. You do not put on a spacesuit. You think the air is like Earth's.

The planet is like Earth but the gases are not quite right. There is life here! You see jungle-like growth. Just then a huge reptile-like thing comes out of the jungle. It is the size of a house. It is like the dinosaurs were on Earth millions of years ago. It has huge teeth. It wants to eat you for lunch. You turn to run back to the ship. Then you fall over. You feel odd. The air on the planet makes you sick.

Do you have the Ril CAT FORCE? If you do (check Equipment List), go to 93. If you do not have the CAT FORCE go to 14.

## 26

You find nothing. You are lost in Null-space for all time.

## 27

The red laser lights meet. There is a big ball of light. Spod says, "Damage to the hull." Lose 5 Life Points as the air goes out of the ship. Now go back to 70 and try again.

## 28

You will visit Aaan on her ship. You get into your spacesuit. You step into the air lock. Then you put the safety line on. The air lock door to space opens. You use the rockets on the spacesuit. Soon you are flying across the space between the two ships. Spod is left in your ship. He is not happy, but he has to look after the ship.

You go past the Ril ship's air lock. You take off your spacesuit. Aaan is there to meet you. The Ril looks down at you. Aaan's cat-like eyes blink from left to right, not up and down like human eyes. Aaan holds up her hand.

The claws on all six fingers are out. Then the claws go in. This is the Ril greeting for peace. You put out your hand and take hers. You tell Aaan that this is the Human greeting.

You go to the control room. You sit on the floor on soft seats. Aaan says "I can give you some 'Marf' or some 'Torg'." You do not know what Marf or Torg are! Aaan tells you that they are like tea or coffee in Human terms. If you take Marf — 77, if you want Torg — 86.

## 29

Spod is still trying the code. Too late! the BLACK SHAPE lets off the H-bomb. You, and all around are blown up!

## 30

Your ships speed into the attack. Lasers blaze away.

THE BLACK SHAPE'S GUNS
FIGHTING SKILL 25

If you win — 85. If you lose — 107.

## 31

You fire at it with a laser. There is a big bang! The hole does not change at all. What next? — 92.

## 32

You fire the rockets at the right time. You shoot round the side of the planet. The gravity acts like a sling-shot and you are flung into deep space. Go back to 122.

## 33

Where will you go? You can hyper-space:
Back to Earth's Solar System — 116
To the Star in the Message — 66
Put in any old code and hope for the best — 100
Try the nearest star system. This was the first plan — 57.

## 34

Aaan makes a growl like a lion or tiger. You feel a burning pain in your head. Then nothing. It has failed. Lose 3 Life Points. You can go back to the Fleet — 72, or try again — 110.

## 35

You just missed the other ship. The SPACE VETERAN heads back to the Fleet. You cannot think why he does not like you. Spod is just happy to be alive. He keeps saying he is alive. He keeps singing "No. 5 is alive! No. 5 is alive." He tells you that this is to do with some old film. It was about a robot in the 20th Century, almost 100 years ago. You tell him to give you some peace.

At last you report to the Fleet. You are told that you will be 2nd in command. Will you choose the Scout Fighter Force — 23, or the Protect Fighter Force — 12?

The main Fleet are very pleased with you. All of the Fleet, both Ril and Human, has the High Council in charge. The High Council has wise Ril and Humans in it. The High Council tells you that, because of the death of Commander Hibbs, you will become the leader of all the Fighter Force. You will become Commander by right, not just in battle when you had to take over as second in command. You are given the rank of 1st Commander. Add 4 Life Points to your Life Points Score. Aaan is given the rank 2nd Commander. Spod is given a medal for his help with the BLACK SHAPE. If he meets anyone he waves it about with one of his arms — 37.

## 37

It is time for the Fleet to find a new star. The Fleet will need to find some more planets. Which star will have planets that will be good for life?

If you have the MESSAGE from the GAS GIANT — 15, if you do not have the MESSAGE — 53.

## 38

The ships have a long shape, with odd marks on them. You know them well! They are Ril ships. The Ril had a war with Humans and you met them in "Space Pilot!" You can attack at once — 20, or report what you see to Commander Hibbs — 91.

## 39

You go to the Moon of the GAS GIANT. This is a bit like the moon Titan in our Solar System (see "Space Pilot"). You see some odd marks on the surface of the moon. You land to see what they are. You and Spod go out to look at some blocks of stone. There was once something here. Nothing lives here any more. You see a large stone house. You can look inside — 76, or go back to 122.

## 40

You take out your laser. You blast the face. It is on a film screen. It was not real at all. The whole screen blows up. You hope that it was not saying anything you needed to hear. You go back out of the SHAPE and back to the main Fleet — 36.

## 41

Commander Hibbs is very pleased to see you. He says that he knows you will be a good pilot. "No one can do as well as you at Space School without being a good catch for a unit" he shouts in a loud voice. Commander Hibbs is only small but he has a loud voice. He always seems to be shouting, even when he is just talking.

"There is a strange comet passing us," he screams. "I was just going to send one of the others to look at it. You can go if you want."

You shake out your ear-drums. Will you take a look at the comet? — 84, or let someone else go? — 16.

## 42

You tell all the ships to put on full thrust. The BLACK HOLE sucks at the ships. Are you too close? Will you have the power? Throw your dice and work out your Fighting Skill Points — 13.

## 43

You agree to the race. You both turn into the meteors. The meteors flash towards you. You turn and twist. You

brake then put on thrust. You speed past the rocks. They make a whoosh! as they go by. Some hit the Force Field.

Throw your dice and work out your Fighting Skill Points — 44.

## 44

Aaan is racing by you. You can see the yellow flashes as the meteors that hit her get burnt up by her Force Field. Can you survive and beat her?

METEOR SHOWER RACE
FIGHTING SKILL 17

It will not be easy. You have to miss the meteors and go fast. If you win — 69. If you lose — 108.

## 45

You turn and face the REPTILE. It opens its mouth. Its vile breath washes over you. Ugh! You feel sick again. The REPTILE slashes a huge claw at you.

ALIEN REPTILE
FIGHTING SKILL 10

If you win — 60. If you lose — 79.

## 46

The hum from the box gets softer. You are moving away from Mass/gravity. Go back to 115 and move again.

## 47

You tell him that you will take up the dare. You both go to the Fighter Ships. Other pilots hear of the duel. They all come along! Go to 64.

## 48

You send Spod to look at the plug-like hole. When Spod gets there he puts one of his own plugs into the hole. Then there is no sound. At last Spod says: "The BLACK SHAPE is a robot. It was sent to seek out and kill those at war with the people of the GAS GIANT'S MOON. It can talk to me. It seems that it is the only one of its kind left. Its masters are long dead. I told it I am a robot too. It did not care. It says that unless we can give it the next code it will blow up. It will use an H-bomb that is inside it! We will all die. It says that we have 2 minutes. I will try to work out the code. There are many codes. Over 1 million. I will start now!"

Spod does not talk now. All you hear is "10010011010 . . ." and so on. Spod can do thousands of codes a second. You hope he is in time! Throw your dice and work out your Fighting Skill Points. Go to 51.

## 49

You see a dark shape and head towards it — 54.

## 50

The Human and Ril Fighters screech into the attack. The lasers' blasts seem to do nothing to the BLACK SHAPE. The SHAPE is a huge box-like thing. It has a high polish. It is smooth and moves fast. The lasers just get turned away from its smooth surface. Two Ril ships and one

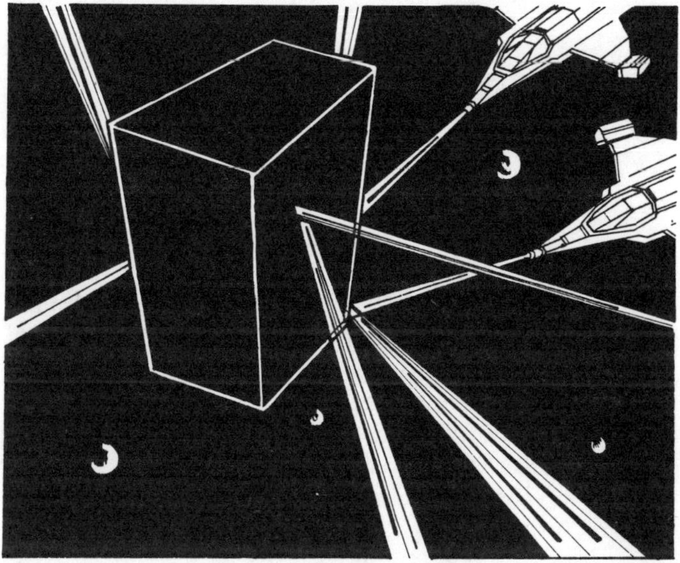

more Human ship are taken out. Now you feel a hum. The Fighters are being drawn into the SHAPE. It is like a magnet. The ships seem helpless! Do you have the numbers from the stone house on the moon? If you do — 94, if you do not — 59.

**51**

The time is running out. You hear "60, 59, 58, 57 . . ." over the radio. The first minute has gone!

BLACK SHAPE DOOR
FIGHTING SKILL 8

If you win — 62. If you lose — 29.

**52**

The spaceships head right at you! — 38.

# 53

The story ends unless you go back for it — 58.

# 54

The dark shape is a planet on your screen. You have found space! You see the stars all around. You still do not know where you are. Spod feeds some new numbers to the hyper-space drive. He hopes that they will do the trick. The ship picks up speed. The speed dial goes over the top. A deep hum fills the ship. The stars are like streaks of light. Then they seem to wink out. You are going faster than the speed of light! You see a ship in front of you!! You pinch yourself. No, you are not dreaming! The ship seems to be one you have seen before. You come up alongside. The two ships are only feet away from each other. You see into the other ship's control room. There is a mad looking robot in there. It is Spod! There is also someone that you see in the mirror every day. This person is looking at you. You look back. It is you!! You have gone into a Time Warp. Somehow it

has made two images of you, Spod and the ship. You wave. So does the other pilot! You will have to get rid of the twin ship if you are to get out of the Time Warp. You turn the ship. You are now heading at each other. There can only be one of you. Who? Throw your dice and work out your Fighting Skill Points to find out — 70.

## 55

You send in Ril and Humans two by two. The BLACK SHAPE has many laser guns. It can fire many at once. It can take out two ships at once. Your ships are shot up! Lose 1 Life Point. Try again — 83.

## 56

The SPACE VETERAN has a lot of tricks. He turns inside you. Your ship is lit up with red light. He has hit you. You have lost! Take 2 Life Points off your Life Points Score. The SPACE VETERAN is still not happy. He comes at you head on! Go to 90.

## 57

You try the next star system. This was the plan. The Fleet hyper-spaces out. There is only one planet in this system. It has no life or air. It is not a good planet. Try again at 33.

## 58

You go to the GAS GIANT. This is a cold planet far out from the sun. It is big and made up of gases. It is a bit like Jupiter in our own Solar System. It has very high gravity. As you get near the planet the radar picks up a "Beep,

Beep". You see a blip on the screen. It is very close to the planet. If you want to go and see what it is — 3, if you do not, go back to 122.

## 59

The BLACK SHAPE will kill you all. You will have to go back and get the code — 39.

## 60

You roll to one side. You can do nothing. Your laser gun does not seem to harm the REPTILE. Then Spod yells, "Duck you bag of bones!" You duck and the ship's laser guns fire. The REPTILE is hit. It goes up in a ball of flame. Its breath was a gas that became flame!

You get back to the ship. You do not know if you will thank Spod for saving you or tell him off for calling you a bag of bones! In the end you thank him. Add 1 Life Point to your Life Points Score. Then you take off! Go to 122.

## 61

Aaan makes a growl like a lion or tiger. In your head you feel like a great cat. You run over a plain after deer. You feel strong and roar like a lion. The MIND LINK is working. Then you hear Aaan in your mind. "This is what we, the Ril, came from. Big cats, not apes like you humans." The pain goes from your head. You and Aaan will now be linked in times of danger. You will be able to tap the force of the big cats. Add 3 Life Points to your Life Points Score. Write down CAT FORCE on your Equipment List. Now you can go back to the Fleet — 72.

## 62

Spod is still trying the code. "10, 9, 8, 7, 6, 5, 4, 3, 2. . ." Spod puts in a code. It is the right one. "Welcome", says the BLACK SHAPE, "You may go in." Just in time. Two seconds to go! You all cheer Spod. Aaan says that the Ril may need something like Spod too. Spod tries to look modest. Lights flash on and off on his head.

Then a door opens in the side of the BLACK SHAPE. If you want to go in — 98. If you want to go back to the main Fleet — 17.

## 63

You do nothing. The BLACK HOLE sucks you and the Fleet into it. You are never seen again.

## 64

The Fighter Ships are docked on the Flagship. Your ship is a TIP24. It has a new Force Field and laser fire (see "Space Pilot!"). You find Spod, your robot, on the ship. He left you to sleep and came back to the ship. He flashes and buzzes to greet you.

The duel will be with lasers set to light. They will show up on the computer when they hit, but will not harm the ship. You both get into your ship and strap down. The other pilot is off at once! A hot flame washes over your ship. The Force Field must work hard to keep your ship cool. He has got away first with this trick. Lose 1 Life Point. Now throw your dice and work out your Fighting Skill Points. Write them on the Adventure Sheet next to SPACE VETERAN. Then go to 102.

**65**

Wrong code! The BLACK SHAPE hits you. Lose 3 Life Points — 94.

**66**

You put in the code that is in the message. All the ships in the Fleet will go into hyper-space. Once again you feel that sick feeling. All is grey as you go out of normal space. Then all the ships pop out of hyper-space.

Something has gone wrong. You are near a BLACK HOLE. This is a star that has fallen in on itself. It has so much gravity that even light cannot get away! It draws in all kinds of things, even planets and other stars. You are not too close, but still the Fleet is slowly drawn in — 80.

**67**

You move away. The two ships flash past each other! — 35.

## 68

You go back to the ship. You make your report. You say that the small, hot planet cannot be used. It is too hot. The warm planet looks fine. The problem here is the air. It is not the right sort for Humans or Ril. It can kill. The planet is also full of huge reptiles. These breathe out deadly fumes and are not easy to kill. This planet is no good. The GAS GIANT has the wrong air as well as too high gravity. The moon has no air. You say that the moon once had air and someone used to live on it. These same persons (or things) seem to have put a message into orbit around the GAS GIANT. The Fleet will have to hyper-space to some other star if it is to find planets for Humans and Ril to live on — 71.

## 69

The meteors whizz past you. Spod says, "Force Field over heating! Oh why did I come on this trip!" You take no notice. You put on full thrust and speed out of the meteor shower. You turn at speed. Then Aaan comes out of the shower. You shoot harmless target light over her ship. You have won! Write down 1 Life Point on your Life Points Score. Now go to 114.

## 70

You see the twin of your ship coming at you. You fire your laser. Red light flashes out of the laser ports. Red light

flashes out of the twin ship's guns too. You turn to the right. The twin ship turns to the left, just like a mirror.

TWIN SHIP
FIGHTING SKILL 20

If you win — 104. If you lose — 27.

## 71

The Ril Commander and Commander Hibbs are talking with other leaders about this. The control panel lights up. Red lights flash. Bells ring. The Fleet is under attack. Bolts of power crash into the Fleet. One of these smashes into the Fleet Commander Flagship. It blows up. In that ball of flames was Commander Hibbs. You are now in charge of the Fleet Fighter Force. What will you do? It is the BLACK SHAPE. The Ril Fleet is under attack too. Take your Fighter Force away from the Fleet — 6. Order Ril and Human fighters to attack the SHAPE — 50.

## 72

You say goodbye to Aaan. You will meet again. You both head back to your Fleets. You get to your Fleet just as you hear a bell ringing over the intercom. It is the warning for the hyper-space jump. A red light flashes on the control desk. Spod yells, "Hyper-space warning! Hyper-space warning! Hyper-space warning!" He also has lights flashing all over him. You tell him to pipe down. "Do something useful, you tin can!" you say. Spod will work out the hyper-space drive sets. You feed the numbers from the Fleet hyper-space control to him. Spod is not happy with the numbers. You tell him to get on with it and not fuss. Spod plugs into the Master computer. You strap down. You press the red button — 73.

# 73

H — Y — P — E — R — S — P — A — C — E, hyperspacehyperspacehyperspace. . . You feel a twisting inside you. You feel a little sick. The control room seems small and you seem huge. Then it seems big and you are tiny. Space and time twist about. The outside is just grey. No stars can be seen. Then the controls chime. A light turns green. You are back in space again. Well, you think you are. The space outside is just black. There should be stars, suns, planets. Spod says "I told you that the numbers were odd!" It seems that someone at the Fleet has given you the wrong numbers. You are lost in Null-space. Null-space is where nothing is. You will have to find a way out.

Do you have the METAL BOX from the comet? If you have the METAL BOX you can go to 115. If you do not you can go back and get it — 81, or try to find a way out without it — 74.

## 74

You can go up — 10, down — 26, left — 49 or right — 103.

## 75

You use the speed that your ship has. The SPACE VETERAN can't match this speed. You turn inside him. The VETERAN'S ship is lit up in green light. It is Spod and your lasers. You have won! Add 1 Life Point to your Life Points Score. The SPACE VETERAN is not happy that you won. He comes at you head on! Go to 90.

## 76

You look inside. There you see a huge black stone. It is in the shape of a long box. It looks like something you have seen. Spod runs the shape in his memory banks. "The BLACK SHAPE!" he says. You see some numbers on the stone. Make a note of them on your Equipment List. They are 1100101. You get back to the ship and take off. Go to 122.

## 77

Aaan brings you some Marf. It comes in a glass. It is cold unlike tea or coffee. It smells like roses. You think it must be a good drink. You take a sip. At once you are sick. The Ril drink does not go down well with Humans! Lose 1 Life Point. Go to 99.

## 78

You send a Ril to look at the plug. He comes back and says "There is a hole, like a plug, in the side of the BLACK SHAPE!" Now what?! — 92.

## 79

The claws just graze you as you duck. You are flung to the ground. The cuts will make you ill later! Lose 5 Life Points. Now go back to 45.

## 80

You can go into hyper-space again — 123, you put full rocket thrust to get away — 42, you hope you will get by — 63.

## 81

Spod says "You will over heat! Take down the thrust." You take no notice. Just before it is too late you come up to the comet. You take down the thrust. You come up to the comet at last. In the ice you see a METAL BOX. You send out Spod on the space sledge. He hacks out the ice round the box. He brings the box into the ship. Write down METAL BOX on your Equipment List. You do not know what it does yet. It has a small sunk-in part. It also has a face with some numbers on it. You turn back to the Fleet. The Fleet is about to move out — 117.

## 82

It is the right code. The BLACK SHAPE gives out a bleep and some other odd sounds. The shine on the SHAPE is now dull. The laser shots seem to go into the SHAPE now. The magnet that pulls the ships into the SHAPE stops. The SHAPE then says "Next code, next code, next code, next code!" You do not have any more codes. You will have to fight on.

"Well," says Spod, "we can hit it now!" — 83.

## 83

You must plan an attack. You can send the Ril in first, on their own — 11, you can send in the Humans first, on their own — 120, you can send in fighters two by two. one Ril and one Human — 55, you can move all the ships around the shape and send in waves of Ril and Humans at the same time — 19, or you can call a meeting — 96.

## 84

You set out after the comet. It has a long 'tail' of dust and rocks. The head of the comet glows. The ships long range probes tell you about the comet. Spod reads from the controls, "Data 011001 0110001 10100 100 011. . ."

"Stop, you tin can" you say, "tell me in English, not code!" Spod tells you that it is time you used some other term, not 'tin can'. He is fed up with 'tin can'. Then he says. "The comet is mostly water, in the form of ice.

There is some odd metal reading. It seems to be a made thing. The metal has been shaped. You will try to get to the comet. It is going very fast. Throw your dice to see if you can get to the comet. Work out your Fighting Skill Points — 106.

## 85

The BLACK SHAPE fires all over the place. There are too many ships for it. Your lasers crash into it. The BLACK SHAPE stays in one bit. The laser guns on the SHAPE keep getting hit. They blow up. At last there are none left. You have won! Yet the BLACK SHAPE is not dead. Your lasers only made the guns blow up. The rest is still there. You will need to get into the SHAPE to see what it is —92.

## 86

Aaan brings you some Targ. It comes in a cup. It steams, and is warm. It smells vile. You choke on the smell. You think that it must not suit Humans. You will have to try it to be polite! You take a sip. It tastes good! The drink has many herbs in it that are good for Humans too. Add 1 Life Point to your Life Points Score. Go to 99.

## 87

Very slowly the ships pull away from the BLACK HOLE. At last you are back out in deep space again. You call Spod and Aaan. What can have gone wrong with the hyper-space jump? You talk it over. At last you work it out. Aaan says "All the star and planets are moving. The universe is moving."

"Yes," Spod agrees, " the Message code that we had was from a long time ago. The star we went to had moved from that place."

"So," you say, " when we put that code into the hyper-space control we went to the place where the star used to be! It has now moved, along with all its planets, in the way all stars and planets do. It was like throwing a ball at a target that moves. We need to think about the moving!"

The three of you work out where the star must be now. The universe moves in a way that can be seen by the right scans. You reset the hyper-space controls. Then into the grey and out again. You are still sick! — 124.

## 88

You tell him that you are going to the control room and have no time. Just then some other pilots go by. They drag you along to the spaceships. They have grins on their faces. They want to see a duel. Go to 64.

## 89

You go to the hot planet. This is very close to the star. It is like Mercury in our own Solar System. You see that it is too hot for any life. Human beings cannot live there. You get too close to the sun. A bit of hot gas comes very close. "Mind my eyes!" says Spod. Lose 1 Life Point as your Force Field has to cool the ship. Now back to 122.

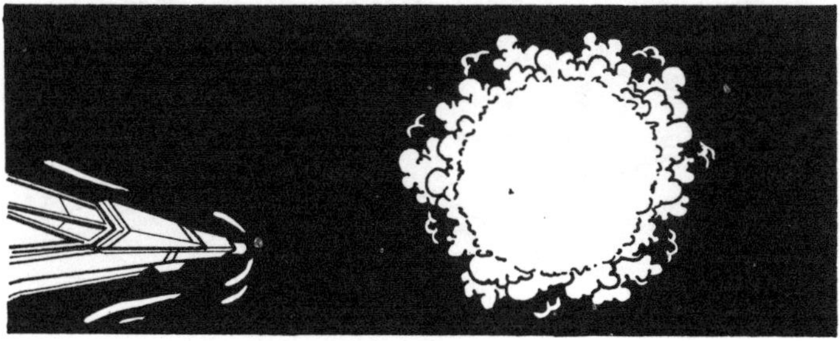

The SPACE VETERAN'S ship is coming right at you. He is coming very fast ! He is going to play "chicken". He wants to see who will turn away in this head to head. The SPACE VETERAN is a little mad. He has had too many years in space. He will ram you! He gets closer and closer. You hear him scream over the intercom. He says "Die, pilot". You hear Spod say "Now for the space robot graveyard in the sky!" Which way will you go? Left — 4, right — 24, down — 111 or up — 67?

## 91

Commander Hibbs comes on the radio. "Do not attack! I say again do not attack! The Ril have made a pact with Humans. They are to come with us to find new worlds. They will help us overcome the BLACK SHAPE." He then tells you to go with the Ril into hyper-space — 95.

## 92

You all fly close to the BLACK SHAPE. It is all smooth as ice. Then you see a small hole in the SHAPE. It is like a plug. You can fire at it with a laser-31, you can send Spod to look at it — 48, you can send a Ril to look at it — 78, or you can send a Human to look at it — 9.

## 93

You feel very sick. The REPTILE is coming at you. You go into the Ril trance that Aaan showed you. You feel the CAT FORCE flow into you. You are strong and quick. Add 2 Life Points to your Life Points Score. Now throw your dice and work out your Fighting Skill Points. You can now add one to your skills. The CAT FORCE helps you. Then turn to 45.

## 94

The BLACK SHAPE keeps sending messages over the radio. You pick up strange numbers. They seem like the code you have from the GAS GIANT'S MOON. You will need to send the code when the same numbers come from the BLACK SHAPE.

Look at the numbers that the SHAPE is sending. Look at the code. Pick the same number.

1000100 go to 119
0110101 go to 22
1100101 go to 82
1100110 go to 65
1100111 go to 112

## 95

You turn and go to the Ril ships. One of the Ril Fighters fires a laser across your bows. You hear a sort of scratchy noise in your headphones. It is a Ril laughing. It then says "So, Human, we meet again." It is Aaan! The Ril you met in "Space Pilot!" We have a little time before hyper-space jump." Aaan says, "Let us test the Speed Kit you have. Come, Human a race!" Aaan does not tell you that she has had the new Speed Kit fitted to her ship.

You both head out into space. Then you see a meteor shower. There are not too many rocks. Aaan is in a mad mood. "Come, Human we will race into the meteors! Have you the skills!?" If you want to race Aaan — 43, if you will not race — 18.

## 96

You call a meeting. As you are all talking the BLACK SHAPE keeps firing. Lose 2 Life Points. Try again — 83.

## 97

The hum from the box gets louder. You are moving to Mass/gravity. You see a dark shape and head towards it — 54.

## 98

You go into the BLACK SHAPE. You take Aaan and Spod in with you. Inside it is all dark. Then a light comes up on a screen. A face looks out at you. It is not like Ril or Humans. It is long and blue. Three eyes look at you. You can take out your laser and blast the face — 40, or wait to see what it does — 109.

## 99

Aaan says that you and she are linked by fate. She tells you that in the distant past of the Ril there were those who were telepathic. They could link minds and pick up each others thinking. Sometimes even now Ril can do this. It is rare and they must take the RIL MIND LINK.

She asks if you will try this with her. Can you link with an alien mind? Will you try the link? If you will — 110, if not — 72.

## 100

You put in a set of numbers. The Fleet hyper-spaces into the middle of a burning star. You all die. Frying tonight!

## 101

You fire the rockets at the wrong time. You speed into the planet at full thrust. You crash and die!

## 102

You blast off into space. You see him a long way off. He turns and comes at you fast! You flip over but he is on your tail. A wash of red light flashes at you. You put on full thrust and it goes by. Spod says "Mind my gyros!". You plug him into the lasers and say "Man that gun, tin can!". Spod tells you that you should have said "Robot that gun."

The duel goes on!

SPACE VETERAN
FIGHTING SKILL 12

If you win — 75. If you lose — 56.

## 103

You find nothing. You are lost in Null-space for all time.

The red laser lights go past the two ships. Both ships fly past each other. Then you turn. The two ships are close now. You crash into the twin ship. There is no crash! The two ships are now one! You are safe. Add 3 Life Points to your Life Points Score. You find the Fleet on the radar scan. You head to the Fleet — 121.

## 105

The story ends unless you go back for it. You will have to go inside the BLACK SHAPE — 98.

## 106

The comet speeds on. You flip on the ship's Speed Kit. The jolt of G-force has your cheeks flopping. Spod says "Mind my gyros!" You tell him that you are fed up hearing about his gyros!

The comet nears the point in space where it will be too far away to chase. You put on full thrust. The 'revs' go into the red.

SPEEDING COMET
FIGHTING SKILL 9

If you win — 81. If you lose — 8.

## 107

The BLACK SHAPE fires all over the place. A lucky hit strikes some of your ships. They blow up in a ball of flames. Lose 1 Life Point. Send in the next wave — 30.

## 108

The meteors whizz past you. Spod says, "Force Field over heating! Oh why did I come on this trip?" You have to slow down so that you can turn away from the rocks. Aaan moves ahead of you. As you come out of the shower she shoots harmless target light over you. You have lost ! Take 2 Life Points off your Life Points Score. Now go to 114.

You wait. The face starts to speak. It is an old film. The face is not real. "Welcome", it says "Know that we, the Blentish race are no more. A deadly enemy has killed us. I am the last of the Blents. We made this robot to kill the enemy. If you are here you will have done well. Know that the enemy came from hyper-space. The place they come from may be found in a message near the GAS GIANT of this star. Know that you can use this message. Feed it into your control data."

Write down MESSAGE CONTROL on your Equipment List.

The face goes on, "Know that the enemy are not like us. The enemy are . . ." The face closes its eyes. It makes a sound as if chalk is scratched on a stone. The Blent is dead. If only it told you more about the enemy. In what way is it not like Humans or Ril? You and the others go out of the SHAPE. You head back to the main Fleet — 36.

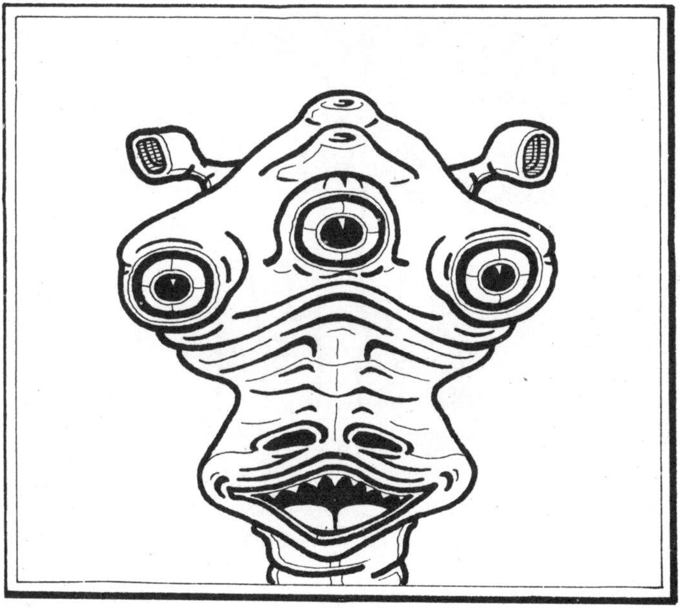

## 110

You say that you will try the LINK. Aaan lights a stick that gives out red smoke. She breathes in the smoke. She then places a helmet on your head. You hear a hum. The helmet feels warm. You link hands and Aaan goes into a trance. You feel a vice-like pain in your head. It seems that your head will burst. Throw your dice and work out your Fighting Skill Points.

RIL MIND LINK
FIGHTING SKILL 10

If you win — 61. If you lose — 34.

## 111

Oh dear! You move down. So does the SPACE VETERAN. The ships smash into a ball of flame. You (and Spod) die.

## 112

Wrong Code! The BLACK SHAPE hits you. Lose 3 Life Points — 94.

## 113

The BLACK HOLE is strong. Some of the ships are pulled in. Lose 3 Life Points. Go back to 13 and throw again. If you have been here before go to 63.

## 114

Aaan invites you to visit her on her ship. If you want to go to visit Aaan — 28, if you do not — 72.

## 115

You take out the METAL BOX. Spod puts a plug into a 10 pin plug he sees. A hum comes from the box. It is to find Mass. Mass is a name for gravity in this case. The box can tell if anything puts a force of gravity on to it. Large things in space do this, like suns, planets and moons.

You can move the spaceship up — 5, down — 46, left — 97, or right — 118.

## 116

The Fleet hyper-spaces back to the Earth star system. They ask if you found a planet to live on. You say no. You have failed. Go back and try again — 33.

## 117

You get to the Fleet just as it is going out. The Fleet will go into deep space. There it will go into hyper-space. This is so that it can travel to the stars. If the Fleet did not go into hyper-space it would take too long. As you get to the Fleet, Spod gives you a talk.

"Now, think about some paper. Put two marks on it, at each end of the paper. Now draw a line between the two marks. This is how long it is in normal space. Now fold the paper so that the two marks touch. Hyper-space is like a fold in space. Now, . . ."

You tell Spod to be quiet. You tell him that you learned all this in Space School. You can also do the maths to show it!

The Fleet is ready to make the jump into hyper-space. You are ahead of the Fleet. You see blips on the radar. Ships closing at speed! You can go and take a look — 2, or take no notice — 52.

## 118

The hum from the box gets softer. You are moving away from Mass/gravity. Go back to 115 and move again.

## 119

Wrong code! The BLACK SHAPE hits you. Lose 3 Life Points — 94.

## 120

The Humans will do as you say, you are the Commander now. The Ril say that the Humans will get all the fun and they want to go too. The BLACK SHAPE sends a laser blast as you talk. Lose 1 Life Point — 83.

## 121

You catch up with the Fleet. Commander Hibbs hears your report. You cannot prove what the VETERAN did to your ship. You will just have to look out for him. The Space Fleet has come out near a star called Alpha Centuri. The sun or star, Alpha Centuri is one of the close stars to Sol. Sol is the sun (star) of Earth. There are three planets at Alpha Centuri. You are told to go and take a look at them — 122.

## 122

You can look at the very hot planet near the sun. You can go to the warm planet. You can go to the huge GAS GIANT planet. The GAS GIANT also has a moon. You can go to this too.

Hot planet — 89
Warm planet — 25
GAS GIANT — 58
GAS GIANT's MOON — 39
To go back to the Fleet when you have been to each one — 68.

## 123

You tell the Fleet to go into hyper-space again. By now you are too close to the BLACK HOLE. You cannot go into hyper-space. You need to be away from any planets, stars or any other type of gravity. Back to 80.

You are in a new star system. The sun has many planets. You scan them all. Only one seems to have the right air. It is not too hot and not too cold. It has water. You take some Fighter Ships out with you to look at the planet. Will it be good for life? Can the Ril and Humans make a home there? Will the enemy that the blue face told you about be there? Will there be other life forms? Will they harm you?

It will be a big job for you as 1st Commander. Find out what happens in the next book,"THE PLANET OF THE TARG!"

## SPACE GLOSSARY

As you can see, there are two lists of words. The first list is called '20th Century'. All of these words can be found in any normal dictionary.
The second list is called '21st Century'. You will not find them anywhere else.

### 20th Century

| | |
|---|---|
| **Asteroids** | Rocks. Some are small and some nearly moon size. Found between Mars and Jupiter in our solar system. |
| **Comet** | Rock flying in space. It goes around the sun. |
| **Gyros** | Something that keeps moving parts stable. |
| **Intercom** | System to talk from ship to ship, or from one part of the ship to another. |
| **Telepathic** | Reading the mind of someone else. |
| **Time Warp** | Going into another part of time. |

### 21st Century

| | |
|---|---|
| **Aaan** | Name of female Ril Pilot. |
| **Blents** | Aliens with 3 eyes. They made the Black Shape. |
| **Hyper-space** | A place between real space. You go into it to travel a very long way fast. |
| **Marf** | Ril drink. It smells good, but makes Humans sick. |
| **Ril** | Cat-like aliens. A bit like Humans, but taller, with six fingers. |
| **Spod 34** | Robot. Thinks like Humans but has huge memory. |
| **Torg** | Ril drink. It smells vile, but tastes good. |

# THE SPACE FLEET ADVENTURE SHEET

Name: .............................................. ....................

Each time you fight you must work out your Fighting Skill Points.

| | | | | |
|---|---|---|---|---|
| You have already been given some Fighting Skill Points for each Fight | + | Throw both your dice and write down the total number you have thrown | = | Add these numbers together to find your Fighting Skill Points |
| Skill Points given | + | Dice throw | = | Your Fighting Skill Points |

You win if you have the same or more Fighting Skill Points than the Creature

You lose if you have less Fighting Skill Points than the Creature.

| Life Points | Equipment List | Story Number |
|---|---|---|
| 25 | | |

| Creature | Skill Points | Dice Throw | Your Fighting Skill Points | Creature's Fighting Skill Points | Win/Lose |
|---|---|---|---|---|---|
| Space Veteran | 8 | + | = | | |
| Speeding Comet | 6 | + | = | | |
| Meteor Shower Race | 13 | + | = | | |
| Ril Mind Link | 6 | + | = | | |
| Twin Ship | 15 | + | = | | |
| Alien Reptile | 5 | + | = | | |
| Gas Giant Gravity | 4 | + | = | | |
| Black Shape Guns | 20 | + | = | | |
| Black Shape Door | 7 | + | = | | |
| Black Hole | 9 | + | = | | |